To Tania

Good luck

Eric.

Let's Get Lost in a Painting

by
ERNEST GOLDSTEIN

EDWARD HICKS
The Peaceable Kingdom

designed by Marsha Cohen

Garrard Publishing Company
Champaign, Illinois

To
Charlie and Gay
and
Amanda Mina Gary
and
Life in
The Peaceable Kingdom

Additional diagrams by Don Stacy

Robert Saunders, Series Consultant

Copyright © 1982 by Ernest Goldstein.

All rights reserved.

Library of Congress Cataloging in Publication Data

Goldstein, Ernest, 1933-
    Edward Hicks' The Peaceable Kingdom.

    (Let's get lost in a painting)
    Summary: Analyzes several of the seventy known "Peaceable
Kingdoms," particularly the 1824 one, painted by the nineteenth-
century Quaker minister, Edward Hicks.
    1. Hicks, Edward, 1780-1849. Peaceable Kingdom—Juvenile
literature. [1. Hicks, Edward, 1780-1849. Peaceable Kingdom. 2
Painting, American. 3. Art appreciation] I. Hicks, Edward, 1780-
1849. II. Title. III. Series: Hicks, Edward, 1780-1849. Let's get lost
in a painting.
ND237.H58A7   1982   759.13   81-20058
ISBN 0-8116-1001-2   AACR2

Editorial and Production services by Cobb/Dunlop Inc.

Manufactured in the United States of America.

Photo Acknowledgments

Edward Hicks, *The Peaceable Kingdom*, The Philadelphia Museum of Art
Entire painting pages 2, 3, 26, 28
Details, pages 5, 7, 8, 9, 10, 11, 12, 19, 21, 23, 25, 29, 36

Richard Westall, R.A., *The Peaceable Kingdom of the Branch*, Free Library of
Philadelphia
page 10

Bewick, *History of Quadrupeds*, The Piermont Morgan Library
page 14

Eugene Delacroix, *The Royal Tiger*, The Metropolitan Museum of Art
page 17

Benjamin West, *Penn's Treaty with the Indians*, Courtesy of the Pennsylvania
Academy of Fine Arts
page 18

Thomas Hicks, *Portrait of Edward Hicks*, Abby Aldrich Rockefeller Folk Art
Center, Williamsburg, Virginia
page 32

Edward Hicks, *Peaceable Kingdom* (1845), Albright-Knox Art Gallery, Buffalo,
New York, James G. Forsyth Fund, 1940
page 33

Edward Hicks, *Peaceable Kingdom* (1827), Friends Historical Library of Swath-
more College
page 34

Edward Hicks, *The Peaceable Kingdom*, Abby Aldrich Rockefeller Folk Art Center,
Williamsburg, Virginia
page 37

Edward Hicks, *The Peaceable Kingdom*, Worcester Art Museum, Worcester,
Massachusetts
page 38   Details: page 39

Edward Hicks, *The Peaceable Kingdom*, Everson Museum of Art, Syracuse, New York
page 40

Edward Hicks, *The Peaceable Kingdom* (1849), Private Collection; photo courtesy Gallery St. Etienne, New York
page 41.

The wolf shall dwell with the lamb
and the leopard shall lie down with the kid
And the calf and the young lion and the fatling
Together, and a little child shall lead them.

Isaiah XI: 6–9

The leopard with the harmless l[amb]
And not one savage beast wa[s]

The wolf did with the lambkin dwell in peace
His grim carnivorous nature there did cease

When the great PENN his famo[us]
With indian chiefs beneath the El[m]

id down
to frown

The lion with the fatling on did move
A little child was leading them in love;

ty made
e's shade.

You are about to enter the Peaceable Kingdom of the American artist Edward Hicks. His kingdom of smiling lions and gentle lambs is a Quaker vision of peace in the world. It is based on the words of the Biblical prophet Isaiah and the deeds of the Quaker hero, William Penn. This painting celebrates that vision of peace in the future and the past. The future vision is when Isaiah's prophecy will be fulfilled: "The lion shall lie down with the lamb." The past celebrates William Penn's historic peace treaty with the Delaware Indians in 1682.

In this book you will look at the Peaceable Kingdom several times. During the journey there will be many questions. The fun and real challenge to you, the reader, will be to answer them yourself. If you do, you will be able to figure out the story and how the artist told it.

You might have noticed that Hicks did something unusual. He explained his work with a poem which he placed on the border of the picture. As you begin your study, do the following:

1. Name the animals.
2. Read the poem starting on your left with the words "The wolf did. . . ." Read clockwise around the painting ending with "When the great Penn. . . ."

THE WOLF DID WITH THE LAMBKIN*
DWELL IN PEACE
HIS GRIM CARNIVOROUS NATURE THERE
DID CEASE

*(BABY LAMB)

THE LEOPARD DID WITH THE HARMLESS
KID* LAID DOWN
AND NOT ONE SAVAGE BEAST WAS SEEN
TO FROWN

*(GOAT)

THE LION WITH THE FATLING* ON DID
MOVE
A LITTLE CHILD WAS LEADING THEM IN
LOVE

*(THE COW)

WHEN THE GREAT PENN HIS FAMOUS
TREATY MADE
WITH INDIAN CHIEFS BENEATH THE ELM
TREE'S SHADE

The animals are in pairs:

1. a wolf and a baby lamb
2. a leopard and a goat
3. a lion and a fatling.

A fatling was any young domestic animal raised for slaughter. Hicks' fatling is a cow. Each pair is made up of a wild animal and a domestic animal. In the Peaceable Kingdom these natural enemies are together. They are resting in peace. The fierce animals have become gentle. The domestic animals are not afraid. The child leads them in love.

In the back, William Penn and the Quakers are making peace with the Indians.

Since the treaty was a solemn occasion, you might have wondered why the Quakers are wearing their hats. The custom of wearing hats goes back to the beginning of the Quaker Movement in England in the 1600s. They refused to take off their hats to other people. They removed their hats only in prayer to God; never to people—not even to the King of England. When William Penn visited King Charles II, he kept his hat on. By this act, he risked persecution. But on that day, the king, with a smile, removed his own hat. Penn was so surprised that he asked the king, "Friend Charles, wherefore dost thou uncover thyself?" The king replied, "Friend Penn, it is the custom of this place for only one man to wear a hat at a time."

William Penn's answer to the King showed another curious Quaker custom: the use of the Biblical words "thee" and "thou" instead of "you." Their use annoyed the English, but these words had a very important meaning. At that time, the English used "thee" and "thou" to speak to servants and maids. Quakers refused to have one language to praise and another to insult. They believed that all people were equals under God. They wore simple clothes and spoke a simple language.

The Quaker Movement was founded in England in the 1600s by George Fox. His first name for the movement was "Children of the Inner Light." Fox believed that all people had an "Inner Light" in their hearts. Since Quakers believe in Christianity the words mean the "Inner Light" of God's love.

Because of their beliefs and customs, Quakers suffered persecutions in England. Since America offered religious freedom to all, the Quakers came to this country. They settled in New Jersey, Delaware, and Maryland.

William Penn founded Pennsylvania, named after his father, as a Quaker colony.

Not much has been written about Penn's Indian Treaty. But it is one of the most important events in our history. You can still see this important document at the Pennsylvania Historical Society in Philadelphia. It is a source of national pride and has meaning to all Americans. It was different from all other treaties because of Penn's regard for the Indians. As a Quaker he believed that the word of God was offered to everyone. He saw Indians as brothers. They were equals under God. He insisted on payment for their lands. He always protected them from the white man's greed and injustice. According to tradition, the treaty was made under the famous elm tree at Shakamaxon. You can identify the figure of Penn in the picture. He is standing with his arms stretched out in a peaceful gesture. He is dressed up for the occasion in his beautiful blue sash.

In the front of the picture you see that same gesture of peace in the outstretched arms of the child. The story up front is the artist's version of Isaiah's prophecy of peace on earth. The world and its inhabitants are at peace: the goat stretches out lazily against the leopard; the cow leans over the lion; and the baby lamb rests against the wolf.

But, wait a minute. Is that a wolf? The poem and the prophecy describe a wolf. Look again. Is it a wolf? The paws and the arch of the back resemble the leopard in front. Also the ears and staring eyes are those of the cat family. In fact, this is a cat. So why a cat when the poem says wolf? We don't know the answer. Perhaps Hicks never saw a wolf. But the wolf/cat raises an interesting problem. Look again and decide which animals seem realistic—as if the artist had seen them. The answer is the farm animals. The lamb and the cow have realistic faces. Their bodies have bones and muscles. Notice how careful Hicks is with the horns of the fatling. They are still baby horns and not the mature horns of a calf.

The wild animals, however, are creatures of the artist's imagination. The lion and the leopard have no bones or muscles. The body of the leopard in front is all wrong. The back is too big. In order to show the oversized paws the leopard has lost its shoulders. The lion is strange. The mane falls over its shoulder like a hairpiece. The face is too long, the nose too big. The body and legs have beautiful curved lines and are in a moving position. But the animal is fixed! It has no movement! It looks like a piece of furniture resting on its giant paws.

Although Hicks had never seen wild animals, he had seen this exact arrangement before. Edward Hicks was born in 1780. He painted this Peaceable Kingdom in 1824. In 1813, the English artist, Richard Westall made a Biblical illustration of the Isaiah prophecy. This picture was very popular in Quaker Bibles in Hicks' time. Look at the two pictures and decide for yourself if Hicks had simply copied the Westall illustration. At first glance, Hicks seems to have made a copy. But when one artist takes from another artist's work, he makes his own creation. This new creation might not be easy to see, but it is there.

Start with the curve of the goat's back. In both works the goat is in the same position. Let's imagine that Hicks saw the graceful sweep of the goat's back and called it the peaceful shape. If you look carefully you will see that

totally relaxed position somewhere in the shapes of all the other animals. You can see this peaceful shape in the powerful arch of the leopard's back; on the curved back of the lamb; on the rounded sweep of the wolf/cat's body; and in the legs and curved belly of the lion. Where else can you find the peaceful shape? If your eye is really sharp, you can see it in the child's arm resting on the lion and in the middle of the tree behind them.

Hicks' Peaceable Kingdom is a visual kingdom. It is a harmony of curved lines and restful shapes. The shapes repeat among the animals, in the child, and in the land. Everything is in harmony and peace. Before going on, let your eye roam through the picture. Can you find shapes in the animals that repeat in the landscape? One good example is the shape of the paws.

How many sets of paws are there? Start on the left with the paws of the wolf/cat. They become bigger on the lion and still bigger on the leopard. If you continue the circle the shape of the paws repeats in the curves of the land in front. *It looks as if Hicks gave the land its own set of paws!*

There is an interesting comparison between Hicks and Westall. Edward Hicks never received instruction in art. He never had a lesson in drawing a body. Richard Westall, however, was a trained artist. But you might have noticed his wild animals do not look real. He drew them as if he had never seen them.

Does it make a difference whether the artist has seen the animals he paints? It is not even clear what is meant by "seeing the animals." Edward Hicks grew up on a farm and knew farm animals. He never visited a zoo and had never seen a real lion, leopard or wolf for that matter. But he had seen them in prints and in books.

Now let's assume that he wanted to study the exact details of a lion. Where would he go? The first place would be to the encyclopedia. His encyclopedia was probably *The History of Quadrupeds* by Thomas Bewick. This book was one of the most famous animal books ever written. Bewick was a well-known illustrator of animals. His work was published in England in 1791 and became very popular in America.

What is so remarkable about this lion is what Bewick says about his drawing. Bewick claims he drew "from a remarkably fine one exhibited in Newcastle in 1788." But it is exaggerated. Bewick's lion tells us that, even as scientists, artists drew animals according to their be-

equally fierce, rapacious, and artful.——At the head of this numerous clafs we fhall place

T H E   L I O N,

WHICH is eminently diftinguifhed from the reft, as well in fize and ftrength, as by his large and flowing mane.——This animal is produced in every part of Africa, and the hotteft parts of Afia. It is found in the greateft numbers in the fcorched and defolate regions of the torrid zone, in the deferts of Zaara and Biledulgerid, and in all the interior parts of the vaft continent of Africa.—In thefe defert regions, from whence mankind are driven by the rigorous heat of the climate, this animal reigns fole mafter; its difpofition feems to partake of the ardour of its native foil; inflamed by the influence of a burning fun, its rage is moft tremendous, and its courage undaunted. Happily, indeed, the fpecies

is

liefs. The best way to understand Bewick's lion is to read his description. His "King of the Beasts" is ferocious and unreal. The drawing has much charm but is not very accurate.

Every artist uses his own style to tell his story and at times he will exaggerate to make his point. You can understand this by looking at the wild animals of perhaps one of the greatest animal painters who ever lived. This man lived in France during Hicks' lifetime. He often went to the zoo to study and draw his animals. His name was Eugene Delacroix.

Below is a lion in the style of Delacroix. Notice the power, movement, and bone structure.

Notice how Delacroix's wavy lines outline the muscles and bones. You can feel the action and movement of the body. Now we will make an imaginative attempt to put a Hicks lion next to a Delacroix lion. In the first illustration we have made a Hicks lion from a Delacroix drawing. The second illustration shows how Delacroix might have drawn the lion in the Peaceable Kingdom.

Notice what happens when Delacroix turns a sketch into a finished work. The drawing on page 17 is a Delacroix tiger. It is exaggerated. Although you see the details, the slope of the body and the rising curves of the back are distorted. The Delacroix tiger is fierce and powerful. We will never again see the big cats as we did before. The artist has done his work.

We have just compared Edward Hicks to several artists, but there is really no way to compare artists. An artist is dedicated to the expression of the beautiful. And every artist sees beauty in his own way. Delacroix, the trained artist and master of detail, created an illusion of power in the cats. Hicks also had a vision. What his eyes had not seen in the flesh, his inner eye created in the beautiful shapes of his animals. Think of Hicks' shapes and the way he repeats them as visual echoes. An echo

repeats a sound; a visual echo repeats a shape. Visual echoes are not accidental. They are part of a careful plan. Even when you do not see them, they are there to please the eye. Once you see the visual echoes in the Peaceable Kingdom, you can begin to understand how Hicks organized his painting. The repetition of the shapes makes it easy for the eye to follow the story. There are echoes all over the painting—echoes of shapes, colors, and ideas. The placement of the animals in front is

an echo of the Westall painting. The placement of the figures in the peace treaty scene is an echo of another Quaker artist, Benjamin West.

West left America and completed this work in England in 1772. Hicks had never seen the original painting, but he had seen copies. In fact, the West painting was so popular that it appeared in Philadelphia on chinaware, on linens, and on tapesteries.

The treaty in Hicks' Peaceable Kingdom is the smaller part of the story and is in back. The prophecy of Isaiah is the more important part of the story and it is in the

front of the painting. The artist wanted to connect two
stories in one painting. The Biblical story is in the future
and Penn's treaty in the past. To show the difference in
time he separates the stories by the use of colors. Look at
the trees in the picture. Can you tell the seasons of the
year?

In the front are the browns of late fall and winter. This is the end of the year. This part of the story deals with the end of time as we know it. It is the end of war and the establishment of God's Kingdom on earth. The colors in the background are the rich greens of spring. Spring is a time of new life, new beginnings. Here the colors are a celebration of a new beginning of peace in the world —the founding of the Quaker colony in Pennsylvania.

The artist's problem still was to tell two stories in one painting. Think of Hicks as a stage director with two dramas—two stories to tell—one more important than the other. The diagram below is an imaginative attempt to make the painting into a stage.

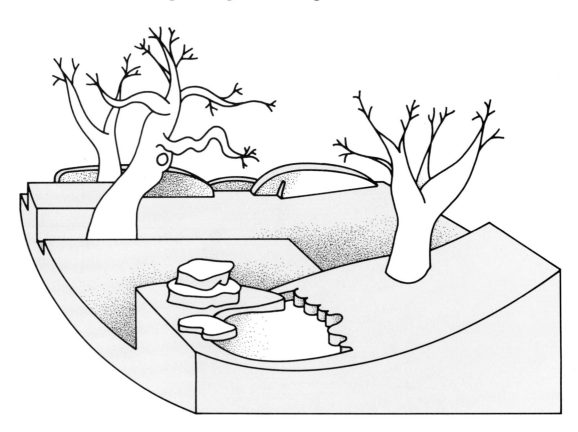

In this way you can see the distance between the future and the past. If everything was taking place on the same level, the groups of figures would be the same size. The Biblical part of the story is shown on a raised platform in front. This increases its size and importance. The historical part of the story, the treaty, is smaller and in back. In this way Hicks solved the problem of importance. He brought together in one painting the Biblical prophecy and the peace treaty. He made the two stories part of the same vision of peace on earth.

It is difficult to tell exactly what is happening in the center of the treaty scene. There is Penn with the Quakers and the Indians. An Indian woman is wearing a leopard skin. That's impossible—there are no leopards in America! It is probably an echo of the leopard's spots in front. There is a man in a red cloak—also impossible! Quakers wore plain clothes. The red cloak, Penn's blue sash and the blue dress of the kneeling figure repeat the colors of the child in front, who is dressed in red, white and blue.

Now look at the detail below. Can you determine what is happening at the center of the peace treaty scene?

It looks like two small children holding a white bolt of cloth. The cloth was payment for the land, but it is the children who are fascinating. The children are echoes of the Isaiah prophecy: *and a little child shall lead them.* In the picture, they are also echoes of the child in front. On closer examination, one child is Indian and the other child is black. An Indian child and a black child are leading the Quakers and Indians in peace. This arrangement tells much about the artist's vision of America. When the painting was done in 1824, slavery existed in the United States. Most Quakers opposed slavery. But there were Quakers who had slaves. Even Hicks' own father had slaves. Among the Quakers, slavery was a burning issue. Most of them opposed slavery yet they were not sure what to do, since they opposed fighting even more. There had also been problems with the Indians. It would be more accurate to say the Indians had problems with the Quakers. Since Penn's time some Quakers had violated the peace treaty, had stolen Indian land, and had cheated the Indians. In Hicks' Peaceable Kingdom all men are united as brothers. It is a kingdom of the spirit, a kingdom for all mankind. That little touch —hardly visible to the eye—tells much about the dream of the artist.

Do you trust what the artist says or what he paints? Before, his poem said "a wolf" but he painted a cat. Here is another brain-buster! Read the last two lines of the poem, "When the great Penn...." Look in the background of the painting and find something different from the poem.

When the great PENN his famous treaty made
With indian chiefs beneath the Elm-tree's shade.

The answer is the tree. According to Quaker tradition, Penn and the Indians made the treaty under the famous elm tree at Shakamaxon. The poem says "beneath the elm tree's shade." But look closely. That is not an elm tree. An elm tree rises gracefully in a Y-shape. It has weeping branches and its leaves are small and round.

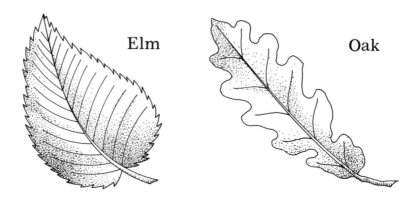

Elm   Oak

The tree over the treaty is an oak. It is easy to identify by its leaves.

The leaves of the oak tree have the same rounded lobes as the tree in the painting. So why an oak when the poem says an elm? The answer is clear. The oak tree served the artist's purpose. Now let's find out why. The oak is powerful. The wood is tough and hard. It lasts and has the feeling of time. This one is a magnificent old oak tree, full of power and strength. As it rises you see two echoes of the peaceful shape—one from the base or trunk and the other from a large branch.

One large branch twists over the treaty scene. Hicks wanted the viewer to pay close attention to this branch. It comes straight out from the tree, twists into a snake-like shape and hangs in the air.

To a Quaker, the word "branch" had a special meaning. The name of the Westall Biblical illustration is THE
PEACEABLE KINGDOM OF THE BRANCH. In this picture there is no branch other than the grape branch in
the child's hand. In Christian religious paintings, the
grape branch meant the blood of the Lord spilled to save
all mankind. In the Hicks painting the branch over the
treaty is an echo of the branch in the child's hand. In the
Bible, branch had another meaning also. It could mean
a tribe or people. Isaiah's prophecy says that out of the

branch of Israel the Redeemer—the Messiah—will come to bring peace on earth. This second meaning is also in the picture. Notice that all of the branches on the oak tree have leaves except this branch. This is the branch of peace—its fruits are the peacemakers below.

There are still more wonders in this marvelous tree. Did you notice the large gaping hole—that gigantic black knot in the middle of the trunk? It has the feeling of an eye. It is an echo of the story in front. Before going on look at the two stories again and try to figure out this echo.

In the lower left corner of the painting a brown line separates the two stories. In the diagram, the line of separation goes straight up—but not to the tree and not to the child. It goes right into the eye of the cow. Now study where the cow is looking. If you draw another line from the cow's eye to the leopard in front, you will have an angle. This angle lines up all the animals. At the center of the angle is the gaze of the trusting cow. Here this obedient animal looks in wonderment at the miracle of peace. The echo of the cow's eye is in the other story. It is the large, rounded, eye-shaped black knot in the middle of the mighty oak! And the peacemakers are lined up beneath its gaze.

Now find the elm tree. If you look carefully, you can see it behind the oak. It rises with its Y-shaped elegance. But the leaves have the wavy lines and the rounded lobes of the oak leaf. But the artist had his reasons for the oak leaves.

Follow the drawing on page 28.

You can follow Hicks' plan easier in the drawing since lines and shapes are lost in the light and shadows. The child, the peacemakers, the animals, the trees, the ground, and the water show up in a simple way—with curved and straight lines.

The wavy lines are on the edge of the picture. They play tricks with the viewer by slowing down the eye. To explain what the artist has done, look at the diagram below. Here are three lines between the same distance. Which one takes the longest to study?

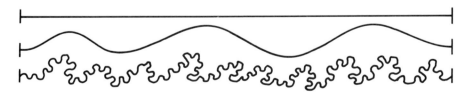

Your eye follows the straight line much quicker. If you follow this idea, you can now understand the reason for the oak leaves. As your eye meets the painting, the stories are told in curved and straight lines. The wavy lines on the edge of the picture slow down the eye and keep you inside the stories. The line drawing shows that the picture requires a great deal of visual attention. You need time to roam through the painting.

And you have spent a lot of time. And because you have, there are still more rewards.

There is a feeling in the Peaceable Kingdom that only comes after time and study. It is a feeling that comes from within the painting itself. After a while, you suddenly see the soft light from the patch of grass. This light fills the entire space. It creates a mood of peace and contentment. The light from within the Peaceable Kingdom is the feeling of the "Inner Light" of the Quaker Movement. It is this special feeling that Hicks gave to his painting.

Hicks created "the mood" from within by his use of color. The light is not coming from outside the picture—for example from the sky. It comes from below—from the ground. The term for this in art is "interior lighting."

The only way to make interior lighting in a painting is to surround it with dark colors. Once again you can compare the painting to a stage. The director has darkened the stage and put a spotlight in the center. The darker the stage the more light there is from the center. In the picture, the dark colors surround the light. The browns and greens are dark colors. On the left are the rich greens of spring; on the right are the deep browns of late fall. The edge of this stage is further darkened by the black and gray-violet of the border. The longer you look, the more you will see how the light rises from the ground. It reflects in the golden yellows of the wild animals and the Indians and it fills the picture with its soft glow. When you have seen this you have finally arrived! You are now inside the Peaceable Kingdom. And you have seen two miracles: one of peace, the other of Edward Hicks.

During his life, Edward Hicks was hardly known—a fact that would have pleased him. He never thought of art as doing God's work. He painted for himself and his Quaker friends. Today, his work is highly praised. A Hicks painting is worth large sums of money. There are more than seventy known Peaceable Kingdoms by Hicks. You can see reproductions of the Kingdoms in books, libraries and in homes. They often appear on Christmas cards. Their mysterious sweetness and warmth belong to the season of peace on earth.

However, Hicks did not have much peace in his life. He was a man with a violent temper. He fought with everyone including his Quaker friends. How strange! Hicks was a Quaker minister, a man dedicated to peace. Yet, he was always in a fight.

Hicks was born in Pennsylvania in 1780—four years after the American Revolution. His father, a British sympathizer, had lost his business. The young Edward grew up on the farm of his Quaker cousins. At the age of fourteen he became an apprentice coachmaker and sign painter. His autobiography tells of a wild youth who spent the nights drinking and brawling. At the age of twenty-two he became seriously ill and almost died. He believed his recovery was a miracle from God. Soon after, he started to read the Bible and joined the Society of Friends—the Quakers.

Quaker religious meetings are quiet affairs. People usually speak only when moved by the "Inner Light." Hicks spoke with such passion that he soon became a Quaker minister. Since this position did not pay him, he continued to work as a coachmaker and painter of signs.

This portrait of Edward Hicks was painted by his cousin and student, Thomas Hicks. Thomas was sixteen, Edward fifty-eight. Before going on, study the face. What does it tell you about the man? (page 32)

The young Thomas knew his subject well. This portrait reveals a man in trouble with himself. It is a study of contrasts between the hard jaw of a fighter and the soft look of a dreamer. The tough features reflect a violent temper. But his eyes tell you much. The eyes have the soft stare of a dreamer. They have the look of the artist's big cats. It is no accident that Thomas included objects of importance to his cousin. In the back there is an open Bible and in his hand a brush; on the easel an unfinished Kingdom with a lion, a leopard and a cow. These three are Hicks' animals. They represent the hard jaw and the soft stare in the portrait. The lion and the leopard represent the arrogant and vicious man Hicks was. The cow is the good and obedient man he wanted to be.

During the twenty-five or more years of painting
Peaceable Kingdoms, these three animals fill up the
space in the front—the most important part of the story.
At times the leopard and the lion smile, but very often

they do not. Over a period of years the expressions on their faces are so different you can read them as a diary of the artist's thoughts and feelings. Hicks was so frightened by his own vicious nature that he often painted himself into the faces of the wild animals. One good example of this is a Peaceable Kingdom in which the lion has Hicks' own face!

As a group of paintings the Kingdoms tell the story of the minister's struggle with himself—to find the peace he did not have in his life.

In the following pages you are going to look at several Peaceable Kingdoms. As you do, you, the reader, should now become the art critic in a very special sense. Study the arrangement of the animals and "read" the faces of the big cats (the leopard and the lion). What human feeling do you find in their expressions?

William Penn

George Washington

Elias Hicks

This Peaceable Kingdom of 1828 is not happy. The animals are not comfortable. There is confusion and fear in the eyes of the cats. The story behind this work was the major tragedy of Hicks' life. In 1827 there was a dispute between the rich and sophisticated Quakers of Philadelphia and the Quaker farmers in the small towns. In a sense this dispute was a fight between the ideas of the English aristocracy and American democracy. The Philadelphians were aristocrats. At their religious meetings, the common man was not allowed to speak. To Hicks, Quakerism meant democracy. All men were capable of finding their "Inner Light"—any man could speak. The painting tells the unhappy story of the dispute. In front, the "paws" of the land repeat in broken chunks of earth. The tree is split and the light is harsh. In the back, the history of the Quaker Movement has replaced the peace treaty. In the middle of the story is the founder of the Quaker Movement, George Fox. Next to him stands William Penn with his arms stretched out in the peaceful gesture. Up front are Quakers bearing a banner telling of Hicks' hope for an end to the dispute. The banner reads, "Peace on earth, good will to men." In the very front dressed in black is the figure of Elias Hicks. Elias was a cousin of the artist and a leader of the dispute against the Philadelphians. In the very center of the group in front is another Hicks hero, George Washington. Washington was not a Quaker, but his place in the picture reveals Hicks' thoughts about the meaning of America. America was founded to be more than another England in the New World. For Penn and Hicks, America was to be a land of religious liberty—"a holy experiment." In this experiment, the golden rule was to be the law of the land. George Washington, as the father of his country, often appeared in Hicks' work. In fact, if you look closely at the child's face in the Peaceable Kingdom of 1824 you can see the image of young George Washington.

But on the other side of the picture, up front, he describes his unhappiness. Hicks had fought with the Philadelphians. He had fought and helped destroy the inner light and the peace of the Quaker Movement. The disappointment with himself is there in the faces of the big cats. They stare out in confusion and anger; it is the confusion of a man angry at himself.

Some of Hicks' most powerful Kingdoms were painted when the artist was troubled. The wild animals are far from peaceful. They represent unhappiness in the world. In his sermons Hicks often used animals to describe people. His speeches explained his Kingdoms. The good people were the gentle lamb, the goat, the cow and the obedient ox. The wicked of the world were the sad wolf, the cruel leopard, the cold and unfeeling bear, and the proud and arrogant lion. These vicious creatures would destroy each other and the world, were it not for the miracle of God's love. Now look at the next painting. Where is Hicks?

This must have been a moment when the burden of being a good man was too much for Edward Hicks. Right up front is the magnificent triangle of ox, lion and leopard. The leopard's face has a vicious look and its beautiful golden color jumps out of the picture. But it is the face of the lion that creates the real mood of the picture. It looks tired; it is exhausted from the heavy weight of that enormous ox! For Hicks, the road to salvation would be heavy and difficult. The entire picture is disturbing. The shapes are not in harmony. The bear and the wolf seem ready to pounce. The child's arm is not resting comfortably on the young lion. The animals are not following willingly; the child now leads them with a yoke.

The next painting is the most disturbing of all.

The animals are crowded—almost thrown together. The faces of the wild creatures are filled with fear and danger. Their eyes stare out from the painting in complete terror. Their look is a cry right from the heart of the artist. What terrible thoughts did Hicks have? Did this lion awake in the middle of a nightmare? Was he paralyzed with the fear that his vicious nature would never change? Perhaps he would never make it into the Peaceable Kingdom?

June 6th, 1981, was proclaimed Peaceable Kingdom Day in Syracuse, New York. On that day, the Everson Museum in Syracuse purchased a most remarkable Kingdom. The price of $200,000 was paid for with funds raised by the entire community. The schools sponsored bake sales; the townspeople and business leaders made contributions.

This painting is considered one of Hicks' very best.

Again, it is not a happy Kingdom. The animals are all
crowded together in a semicircle. And again, it is the
face of the lion that creates the mood of this Kingdom.
The lion is not happy, it is unbelievably sad. His wide-open
and teary eyes, the drooping mouth, and the large soft
mane are weepy. The same feeling repeats in the stare
of the leopard. Sadness fills up the picture. This King-

dom tells the story of a man who has suffered much. Maybe this was when his granddaughter had died. Perhaps it was when he had lost some dear friends from an outbreak of typhoid.

Edward Hicks died in 1849. In his old age he seems to have found some peace. The last Kingdoms are quiet and serene.

This picture was finished a few months before his death. Notice all the animals are now up front. The leopard stretches out in the center. The golden yellows of the cats create a mellow mood. The old lion has lost his arrogance and has become humble as it shares the food of the ox—straw. The child leads the fatling and the ox in procession while the young lion turns for one last goodbye to the world.

Besides the large number of Kingdoms, Hicks painted famous events of American history, Biblical stories, and farm scenes of Pennsylvania. In his heart, the Quaker minister was a farmer—he had even tried farming and failed. However, he continued to work the land with his brush. His paintings open the eyes to the beauties of nature's shapes and the rich color of the Pennsylvania countryside.

From this short study, the Kingdom of 1824 represents a rare moment of peace in Hicks' unhappy life. It is not like any of the other paintings. The shapes blend in beautiful harmonies. The inner light fills up the whole picture with its message of peace and love. Because this is one of the earliest works, it is important to all the other Kingdoms. The solutions he found and the designs he used in this painting repeat in all the others. You have probably found many echoes of this early work in the later paintings. And the more you look, the more you will discover!

As you become more familiar with the different Kingdoms you will recognize they are the same but different. Each one has two stories with a dividing line and certain animals are always in the pictures. But from the positions of the animals and the expressions on their faces, the stories will change.

Once you understand this technique, you can read the Kingdoms as you read the fables of Aesop. Remember when the starving lion roared and then refused to eat his friend Androcles? These same human feelings are in the animal world of the Peaceable Kingdom. The animals are all the people in the world—the good and the bad—and sometimes it is not easy to find yourself. For who has not awakened from a nightmare? Who has not acted with too much pride or anger? Who has not known terrible sadness? And who among us has not prayed to be good? Somewhere in every Kingdom there is hope. Had not the painter of these animals been saved from death by a miracle of God? Surely the Creator of the world loves all His creatures—even the most vicious!

Although the Kingdoms celebrate the miracle of God's love, they are the work of a man who did not have much peace in life. Hicks was a believer who saw much evil and wickedness in the world. He was an angry man with a violent temper. He was a tortured man—a man of faith, with no faith in himself. At Quaker meetings it was the custom to speak only when moved by the inner light. Often the minister remained silent. At other times, Hicks doubted the words of his own sermons. During his life he doubted his worth, his character, and especially his art. But he never doubted his vision. When everything else failed him, he had the Bible and the brush. With his brush he told us everything. Perhaps that is the reason for so many Kingdoms. It is rare for an artist to do the same painting again and again. When he finishes a work, it is done. He will go on to the next painting. But Isaiah's prophecy has not been fulfilled, The Golden Rule is not the law of the land and men still make war. So the Kingdoms had to go on and on until the very end of Hicks' life.

The legacy of the Kingdoms is an amazing achievement. It is amazing because Hicks never received art instruction. He is what we now call an "American original." By trade he was a coachmaker and sign painter who always wanted to be a farmer. By calling, he was a Quaker minister who felt that art was not God's work. How wonderful, how strange! This man who hated art but had to paint. What he painted always told two stories. In one we learn about Hicks, his hopes, his pain. In the other, we see the beauty of God's Creation. The first story shows how life is. The other, the more important story, reveals how life can be in the Peaceable Kingdom.